Building with Strong Materials

Lamar Coldwell

Rosen
REAL
READER

Rosen
Classroom™
New York

1

Architects and engineers build many different structures. They decide what materials to use.

A tent needs to be light.

It needs to be easy to carry.

Cloth and flexible poles are good materials for a tent.

Cloth for a house does not make sense.

A house is not being carried.

It does not get put away.

It needs to last for a long time.

Architects use strong materials for houses.
They use wood, metal, and stone.

The foundation is concrete.

It is a strong building material.

It is made of stone and gravel.

It is made of sand and water, too.

It gives the house a strong base.

There are metal beams.
These beams hold the weight of
the house.

Architects and engineers use strong materials to build skyscrapers.

They use strong materials to build bridges, too.

Bridges need to hold a lot of weight.

Cars and trucks are heavy.

Strong materials are used to build tunnels.

Tunnels must hold the weight of land or water.

Strong materials last a long time. They help buildings stand up against wind and water. What materials do you like to build with?

beam

bridge

foundation

skyscraper

tent

tunnel